My Little Dirt Bike

REVISED EDITION

LEANNA CRAIG LEBATO

ILLUSTRATIONS BY JOSE RAMOS

ISBN 9781730955082
© Copyright 2018 by Leanna Joy LeBato
My Little Red Adventure Books
Houston, Texas

Revised Edition
Printed in United State of America

To Emma, Caden and Audrey.
For endlessly asking about my little red dirt bike.

One bright spring morning, I slipped on my favorite pair of sandals and grabbed the red leash. Jammin', my dog, heard the leash make a jingle sound and came running.

She kept running and didn't slow down. She began sliding … sliding … BOOM!

She crashed right into me, knocking me to the ground. Her yucky, dog slobber was stinky and super gooey. As I wiped my face I heard a deep rumble sound, and I knew it was Dad's truck.

"Hey Dad," I called as I walked outside.

Then...I saw it.

I froze with my mouth hanging open.

It was small and red... it just couldn't be!

Jammin' excitedly jumped into the truck bed sniffing it over.

"Is this real?" I asked.

"Yes! It's a 50cc ... a dirt bike!

I always wanted one of these when I was your age," Dad said

"This is awesome!" I shouted. "Can you take me for a ride?" "I sure can," he said. "But first, let me take it for a spin and check it out."

It was unbelievable ... a real dirt bike!

It wasn't shiny and new, but I didn't care. It was small, red and it looked like the tires had several miles on them. But it was going to have a new life with me.

I imagined the places I could go.

I could ride around the pond in the big pasture behind my house.

I could ride out to the wild black berry patches.

I could ride to my friend Leigh's house.

I watched Dad as he rode down the street, and turned around to come back and get me.

Finally, he was back. "Hop on! Hold on tight!" he said. Before he could finish his sentence I jumped on.

We were off.

Jammin' started chasing after us. The wind was blowing through my hair.

I was cold, with goose bumps forming on my arms, but it didn't bother me because I was riding a dirt bike!

Over the next few weeks Dad taught me how to steer and use the brake.

The hardest part of riding was learning how to switch gears.

It had three: the first gear kept me going very slow, the second I could go faster, and in third I could go even faster, reaching thirty-five miles an hour.

With lots of practice, I learned how to shift, and every day after school I rode my little red dirt bike until the sun set.

Summer finally came and it was hot, but it wasn't too hot to ride.

When I went fast I didn't feel the heat, just a warm breeze. As I rode around the yard again and again it began to make dirt trails.

When the cows were not around I opened the pasture gate, and rode around the marshy pond.

One day I rode further out to the wild blackberry patches and picked fresh berries.

I brought the berries home and Mom helped me make a blackberry cobbler. It was delicious!

Jammin' willingly cleaned up all the crumbs I dropped.

But that night I forgot to close the pasture gate, and the next morning our backyard was filled with cows.

Dad made me herd them back to the pasture. Jammin' eagerly helped.

One morning I rode to my friend Leigh's house. We rode around her front yard. She was smaller than me, so we could easily ride double.

We made up a dirt bike game. Leigh closed her eyes, held on tight, and had to guess where we were riding. It was a little scary, and made our tummies tickle.

We rode to the creek to hunt for turtles.
We carried them back to her house in a bucket.

Then, we put them in her greenhouse with the other turtles. It was an old, warm building with clear plastic walls, about the size of a small room.

That was the best summer ever.

I grew to love my little red dirt bike.

Small 50cc, Red Dirt Bike for sale $150

As the years went by I grew taller, and my little red dirt bike I loved became too small for me.

My dad said, "It is time to move on. It is time to sell it".

He put an advertisement online that read, "Small 50cc, Red Dirt Bike for sale $150."

One day I came home from school and it was gone. I couldn't believe it. I felt so gloomy that Mom thought I had the flu.

Jammin' must have been sad too. I tried to take her for a walk, but when she heard the leash make a jingle sound, she didn't come.

That weekend Leigh called and asked me to come over to her house to play.

When I got there she said, "I have something to show you."

Together, we walked outside to her shed. Jammin' trailed closely behind us.

All weekend we rode the little red dirt bike. It was a tight squeeze for us to fit, but we didn't care.

We rode around her yard. We rode down to the creek to hunt for turtles.

We rode and played our guessing game.

We rode until the sun set.

AVAILABLE NOW!

My Little Red Jalopy

My Little Red Camper

About the Author:

Leanna enjoys writing stories about her adventurous childhood. When she is not writing, she enjoys photography, playing ukulele, and spending time with her family.

About the Series:

My Little Red Adventure Books was inspired when Leanna's children discovered an old photograph of her riding a dirt bike.

They never knew their Mom was once free spirited and adventurous. They only knew her as "Mom." They began to ask her tons of questions about her dirt bike and her childhood adventures.

Instead of just telling them the stories … she began to write them down.

Made in United States
Troutdale, OR
11/24/2023

14894167R00021